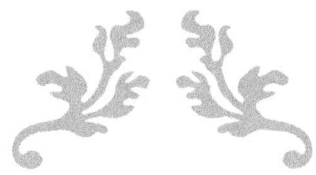

WHAT'S NEXT?

Strategic Marketing For Authors

PATASKITY PUBLISHING CO.
207 Hudson Trce Augusta, GA 30907

Copyright © 2019 by Ana Aliceia Blair. All rights reserved. No part of this publication may be reproduced, stored in a retrieval system, or transmitted in any form by any means, electronically, mechanical, photo-copying, recording or otherwise without written permission of the copyright owner.

ISBN-13: 978-1-948605-05-2

ISBN-10: 1-948605-05-8

PATASKITY PUBLISHING CO.

207 Hudson Trce Augusta, GA 30907

Suite 102

TABLE OF CONTENTS

INTRODUCTION 7
CHAPTER 1 10
TEN MARKETING STRATEGIES FOR NEW WRITERS 10
CHAPTER 2 14
   THINGS TO CONSIDER WHEN CHANGING YOUR
   MARKETING STRATEGY AS AN AUTHOR 14
CHAPTER 3 16
   TEN TIPS FOR SUCCESSFUL COLLEGE MARKETING 16
CHAPTER 4 19
   PUTTING LINKEDIN MARKETING TO WORK 19
CHAPTER 5 22
   SEO TRAINING 22
CHAPTER 6 24
   AFFILIATE MARKETING 24
CHAPTER 7 27
   VIDEO MARKETING STRATEGIES 27
CHAPTER 8 29
   UNCOVERED STRATEGY TO GET FREE RADIO
   PUBLICITY THAT REALLY WORKS 29
CHAPTER 9 31
   TELEVISION MARKETING STRATEGIES 31
CHAPTER 10 34
   RADIO MARKETING STRATEGIES 34
CHAPTER 11 37

A STRATEGIC PR PLATFORM FOR SPONSORSHIPS, TV APPEARANCES AND OTHER EXPOSURE 37

CHAPTER 12 39

BE PUBLISHED IN THE NEWSPAPER 39

CHAPTER 13 42

SECRETS TO AFFILIATE MILLIONAIRES - 5 AFFILIATE MARKETING STRATEGIES FOR YOUR SUCCESS WITH LOW COST 42

CHAPTER 14 47

TWENTY ECONOMICAL BOOK MARKETING TECHNIQUES 47

CHAPTER 15 52

WHAT MAKES A GOOD BOOK MARKETER? 52

CHAPTER 16 55

FIVE SUCCESSFUL MARKETING STRATEGIES FOR FICTION AUTHOR'S 55

CHAPTER 17 60

COMMON MISTAKES AUTHORS MAKE ON INSTAGRAM 60

CHAPTER 18 64

WHAT'S NEXT? 64

INTRODUCTION

This is the strategy that ninety-nine percent of bestselling self-published and indie authors used to become successful. I must warn you that because this strategy is so incredibly simple that it might seem "too easy" or "too obvious." I would urge you to set aside such notions and first seek to fully understand the strategy, and then apply it. Test it for yourself. You will be amazed by the results you see even though the strategy is so very simple.

Create Massively Valuable Content Regularly for Your Audience.

The key foundation to the ultimate author marketing strategy is that you must create massively valuable content regularly. There are many, many ways you can do so, but any strategy will work as long as you follow the three key principles of this approach:

1) Provide Massive Value

We are not talking about a little bit of value – we are talking about MASSIVE value. Massive value means that your content makes a difference in someone's life. After indulging in your incredible content, your audience should feel inspired, educated, or thoroughly entertained. They should remember the experience of reading your content for days, weeks, months and even years to come in some cases. The way you present this value is up to you; however, there are various ways for you to provide your audience with content ongoing. We will discuss oppurtunies such as social media, Search Engine Optimization (SEO), blogging, websites and much more. These are all forms or outlets which you can use to provide your audience an ongoing massive amount of information. Thus, keeping your audience engaged and interested in your writing.

2) Provide It Regularly

Nowadays, everything is so fast paced. Because of our fast-paced world, it is no longer just enough to give people a wonderful book, or a wonderfully entertaining video once. You must be regularly providing amazingly valuable content for your audience. "Regularly" should be at a minimum weekly for most forms of content, but it might be daily or monthly depending on how easily and quickly it can be produced.

3) Create Value for YOUR Audience

Finally, you must create this incredible value for your audience – not random people who may or may not even care about your books or what you do. You want to create massive value for your audience who will be likely to purchase your books and share them with others.

For example, if you write about business, you ought to be creating content that is interesting and valuable to people interested in business. If you write young romance novels, you should be creating content that's valuable and interesting to people who read young romance novels. Writing romance novels and creating educational videos about business will not help you become a bestselling novelist. Make sure your value is a match for your audience!

Content Creation Options

There are many kinds of content you can create and even more ways to distribute this content to your audience. The key is to pick one kind of content and only one distribution strategy and become the absolute master of that channel.

CHAPTER 1

TEN MARKETING STRATEGIES FOR NEW WRITERS

In business, success hinges on a successful marketing campaign. This also applies to new writers who want to take their talent of writing and make a profitable business with it. To help new writers who may know nothing about marketing and business, here are ten marketing strategies for new writers.

1. Make Your Site Reflect Your Writing Style

This is a unique marketing strategy for writers. When people search for writers, they often judge the content on their website. The potential clients are looking for a certain style that matches their vision. Therefore, always use your own style of writing when creating content to promote your business; do not simply rewrite other writer's content.

2. Create An eBook

Create a free downloadable eBook that potential clients can read. The main goal of your eBook should be to provide writing samples and help your clients understand your full abilities. You may write short fiction stories, or you may write in-depth technical articles. It mostly depends on the type of clients you wish to attract.

3. Use Agency Sites

Starting out, not many people are going to know you are a talented writer. You should greatly consider joining an agency site that acts as a middle man, connecting writers with clients. Once you build a client list, focus on your own site, and ask your clients to promote you to their friends who need writers.

4. Create A Full Bio

Before people do business with other people, they want to know with whom they are doing business. Create a full bio on your website; make sure you include pictures, location, contact information, reviews and other important information.

5. Create Business Cards

There are plenty of brick and mortar business owners than can use the help of a writer. Many writers construct public relations articles to help their client's image. You should give everyone you meet a business card, and let them know what type of writer you are and how you can help them achieve their goals.

6. Promote yourself on social media sites

Social media marketing is unarguably one of the best marketing methods. Every social media site has pros and cons, so be sure to create an account on each major site, such as Facebook, Twitter, Google+ and even YouTube. Experiment to see how each site can benefit your business.

7. Use Articles

Write and place articles on high-quality article directories. High-quality article directories are usually directories that do not compensate their contributors in any way; this cuts down on the amount of low-quality or spam articles. Make sure you link back to your site in the articles you submit.

8. Network

Do not be afraid to meet new people. You never know who will come along, and greatly help your business succeed. By constantly meeting new people, you can exponentially increase your customer base. Your business depends on the relationships you make with people.

9. Post Ads

Take advantage of free ad sites, such as Craigslist. You may even want to post ads in the local paper. Many people still search classified ads to find services.

10. Create A Google Business Listing

If you want to take your writing to the next level, create a free business listing on Google. Make sure to include important information that can help your listing reach the top result for your industry in your area. People who search for freelance writers in your area can come across your business listing and contact you for your services. Take advantage of these ten marketing strategies, and eventually, you will grow and you will not need to do so much marketing.

CHAPTER 2

THINGS TO CONSIDER WHEN CHANGING YOUR MARKETING STRATEGY AS AN AUTHOR

If the mere thought of overhauling your marketing strategy gives you anxiety, I get it. It's time-consuming. There's a lot of hard work involved. And, of course, there's always the risk that the new strategy will sink your business, decimate the lives of everyone you love and reduce all of your hopes and dreams to ashes.

Alright, changing marketing strategies is not that scary, but it sure can be daunting. And while it might be tempting to avoid the trouble altogether and stay the course, sometimes a change is necessary.

If you're an author due for a change, take a deep breath. This book will be of help. Now then. To ensure your new strategy is best positioned for success, I've outlined four important considerations below.

How to Know When to Change Strategies

The question of when and how often writers or authors should update their marketing strategy is related to a whole variety of forces which includes, but are not limited to:

the industry, target buyers, market trends, sales cycle and other specific needs. That's why you need to create a structure to plan, track and reassess your strategy, tweaking and potentially overhauling as warranted.

For many that system looks more or less like this: Build a detailed strategy designed to achieve your goals. Monitor your results. Quarterly reviews are an excellent opportunity to review your goals, tactics and the outcome of your efforts to make sure you're on track to hit your milestones.

Think small. Monthly reviews are a great way to keep individual channels on track. Reviewing your efforts on a monthly, and quarterly basis will help you determine if a strategy shift is in the cards. Keep in mind that changing the direction of your marketing strategy is not a decision to make lightly. After all, careful planning alone takes a lot of time, not to mention the hours and costs spent on implementation and potential lost revenue as you work to establish a footing in new areas. More importantly, when the change is significant, the effects will ripple through.

CHAPTER 3

TEN TIPS FOR SUCCESSFUL COLLEGE MARKETING

1-Advertise On Facebook

Use Facebook! Facebook is the average college student's first choice. I even find myself feeling the need of Facebook withdrawal from time to time. Everything on facebook seems neccessary, from the useless profile of each and every student to the never-ending lists of groups available. Facebook is constantly growing and expandine. So, you may want to ask yourself: "Why not join the fun?" It is one of the best marketing tools to reach college students.

2- Make It Funny

The attention span for the average college student is an estimate of thirty seconds (give or take). If it is not interesting, it is not going to be abosorbed. Funny is always interesting. Funny means the student can go home to whoever and retell it; making the student seem "cooler," and therein receiving even more advertisement through heresay.

3- Don't Buy TV Ads

While television ads are a great way to adverstise, the average college student does not have time to watch tv and usually might not even own a tv. It's a waste of money and effort if your targeted audience are college students.

4- Unique / Original

Referring back to the small range of college student attention spans, if they've seen it before, there is no point in paying attention.

5- Free

My favorite words in college were "cancelled," "postponed," and best of all "FREE." "Free" is the one word that can grab any college student's attention, no matter what the context; free food, free day, etc. Students (and former students) will do just about anything to get something for free or save $2.

6- Contests

Winning is always fun, and giving the opportunity to win anything, is good enough for the average college student. Contests are interesting and attention grabbing; always a good approach.

7- School Newspapers Are A Waste Of Money

Unfortuently, not many college students read the school newspaper (goes back to the whole time restrction and attention span points). Even the ones who do read will most likely spend very little time perusing through the ads. School newspapers don't really shout out efficacy.

8- Sponsor Organizations

One thing college students love is money. Helping out student organizations that they care for will win major brownie points and could help in swaying the attention of the student.

9- Ditch The Flyers

In college, flyers are used for bedding for your pet, toilet paper, scratch paper and maybe blankets for the homeless.

10- Ask The pros

And by Pros I mean the students aka, shameless plug, college students who can assist you in getting the word out. anyways at least ask students what they want and go on campus and observe. When you observe, connect and offer value it becomes easy to build relationships.

CHAPTER 4

PUTTING LINKEDIN MARKETING TO WORK

When it comes to online marketing, most authors often first think about search engine rankings, back linking, and perhaps even social media marketing. When social media marketing comes to mind, many authors often think about sites like Facebook and Twitter. Of course, there are many other social media sites that you could be putting to work for you, too, and among the tools you may not be considering, but should be, is LinkedIn marketing.

Why Use LinkedIn?

What many people do not understand about LinkedIn is that it is more than just a basic social media site. It is designed to help professionals connect with other professionals, but it also is a search engine of its own. Because of this, it has great ranking power when it comes to its own links being found on other popular search engines like Google. With this in mind, you can see that LinkedIn marketing can be used with great results to boost the visibility of your own sites if you use the site in the most optimal way.

Revising Your LinkedIn Profile

When many people set up a LinkedIn page, they use it as a digital resume of sorts, but what few people know is that you can actually edit some of the tabs on your profile. Those links that state "My Website" and so forth can actually be customized. You can use keyword optimization strategies here combined with the power of LinkedIn marketing to optimize rankings to your great advantage. Rather than use "My Website," you can alter that wording, and put keywords that are associated with your website to boost your visibility.

Starting Groups On LinkedIn

Another great benefit to you for your LinkedIn marketing efforts is the ability to create a Group on this social media site. You will want to choose a strategic name for your group so those interested in what you are offering can locate you. Then you can start by offering those who are already your contacts to enter your group. As the group moderator, you will want to include plenty of your own valuable content, pose interesting or thought-provoking questions, and more so that others are encouraged to participate. The benefit of groups is to establish new relationships, promote messages in various ways, and more.

LinkedIn Marketing Benefits

The unfortunate fact is that when it comes to social media marketing platforms, LinkedIn is perhaps one of the most under-utilized tools today. It is a platform with many members; however, and these members are there for you to develop relationships. Most people on this site are interested in growing their network by not only maintaining relationships and keeping in touch but also in establishing new relationships, too. When you know how to properly leverage this site and put its benefits to use for you, you can really enjoy some great benefits that you will not be able to enjoy from working with other sites like Facebook and Twitter. If you have not looked at LinkedIn marketing recently, you may find that you can truly benefit from what this site has to offer.

While most marketers ignore LinkedIn Marketing, it is an absolute gold mine for leads, potential customers and potential business partners.

CHAPTER 5

SEO TRAINING

If you are a new online business owner, what should you keep in mind when developing your marketing strategies? In order to be effective, you should focus on developing high quality content and diversifying your link sources. The search engines continue to be one of the primary sources of traffic for most business owners online, and this is unlikely to change anytime soon. You need to be aware of the current algorithm changes and what may be coming in the future; however, including how Google and other search engines use the quality of your content in order to determine search engine rankings. It seems Google is putting more emphasis on originality, length, and latent semantic indexing.

In other words, Google is rewarding websites that have longer, more meaningful articles that are unique (instead of using the exact same text or very similar on many other websites). Perhaps the best long-term strategy you can develop for search engine optimization is to create the best content you can with your visitors in mind. Try to create that type of content that deserves to be at the top of the search results -- the kind of content that your visitors might naturally link to --

even if you realistically still have to do a lot of promotion yourself.

Link building is still the key for search engine rankings. Getting inbound links to your website still continues to be one of the primary strategies for improving your search engine rankings, and this is unlikely to change anytime soon. Please be aware, however, that the standard ways of building links may become less effective over time, so you have to focus on diversification. Instead of relying on the same websites over and over, it is best to get inbound links from as many different websites as possible.

Also, be careful with shortcuts like automated software tools that build hundreds or even thousands of links in a short time. This is certain to raise a red flag with Google and other search engines, and your rankings may suffer in the future for these practices (if they haven't already). One example is article submission software that sends out your content to thousands of directories at once. For one thing, you have to be careful with building links too quickly like we already mentioned (especially if you're promoting a brand-new website). It's also best not to use the same article when submitting to so many different directories. Even if this doesn't get you penalized, per se, it would likely be far less effective than submitting unique versions to various directories.

CHAPTER 6

AFFILIATE MARKETING

"With Affiliate Marketing, anyone can make money online easy and fast!" That is a statement most often misused and seem to get people's attention for a way to make money on the internet. Yes it does sound real good. However, you should ask yourself: "How true is it?" For many people it's not and yet for others, it is. Well, why is that?

There are a number of things to take into account if one decides to enter the field of Affiliate Marketing. It's easy enough to get started if you know the basics of how to operate a computer, write some documents using an editing or e-mail program and surf the internet. It's after that, where a number of people continue for a bit and then decide to give up. This mainly occurs when they need to write information about the product that they are planning to promote for sales.

For instance, writing blog postings and articles is a bit of a stumbling block for many people at first. It's not hard if you already know a bit about the product or topic. To overcome this block, you can surf the web and get the information about what you're intending to promote. From there, formulate some articles in your own words about the item or topic. This may take a little time to accomplish.

You'll also need a Domain Name (web site name) and a place that will host it for you. Some affiliate marketers choose just to use their blog as a site whether it be for one product or several. While this may work OK for some, it may not produce the income results that many are thinking of getting. A number or product owners have ready made sites that you can copy and use or special links to use for access.

With affiliate marketing, its up to you to get the traffic to the site or sites in order to make the sales and get paid a commission of the product. This is done when you write information and make it accessible to others online. There are some guidelines that have to be followed or these places will not publish your information. How fast you start making money depends on how fast you get your information out to the eyes of interested readers and get them to your site. For some, making money in affiliate marketing can happen in as little as a couple of weeks.

To get off to a good start in Affiliate Marketing, it helps a lot to get some good training. Amazingly enough, there are web sites and tools to help that you can get for FREE! You can get started with your Domain Name and Hosting for less than $10.00 and from there it can pay for itself while putting some great money into your pocket, month after month.

CHAPTER 7

VIDEO MARKETING STRATEGIES

If you're not including video marketing as one of your strategies, your missing the boat! Here's why... Its the only marketing method that puts you right out in front of people and makes you real to them. Its the top way to brand your face and voice, people are more willing to buy or join up with a person who has a face and voice to them. Your not just an ad somewhere in internet land, this allows you to break the credibility gap while increasing your sales conversions.

Many sources say video marketing will be eighty-five percent of all the traffic online; therefore, eventually you'll be forced to learn video marketing strategies, whether you like it or not! The top problem people have with video's is they don't know what to say, or in what format to actually be effective with it.

Thereis a formula for conducting all videos, no matter the niche! This well help you create videos which convert to targeted and qualified traffic immediately.

First you need a very powerful opening statement, which includes the problem your going to solve for them. This will hook them to stay, instead of clicking their back-button. Your opening statement should be like a headline on a squeeze page. "Stay tuned because I'm going to show you exactly how to generate targeted traffic with video marketing strategies no one uses but me." Get the point? After that you want to talk a little bit about your background and who you are. Make sure to make it in relation with what your about to talk about, this will brand you and give you authority in what your saying.

Once you have done that, now you can talk about the solution. You should sell the hole not the drill. What I mean by that is do not talk about your product or service features, talk about how their problem can be solved. Once you've established how they can solve their problem, give them a call-to-action! This can be your website, your phone number or maybe your email. It all depends on what your trying to accomplish. Send people to a targeted website where the can get the solution discussed in the video.

CHAPTER 8

UNCOVERED STRATEGY TO GET FREE RADIO PUBLICITY THAT REALLY WORKS

Authors who have published a book will quickly move into needing to secure publicity for as low cost as possible. There is an opportunity that you can take advantage of to receive free or low cost radio advertising, and it really works. It begins with the fact that there are twenty-four hours in a day, and seven days a week; This is a lot of time for radio stations to fill. Not only fill, but fill with valuable content. Therefore radio stations seek outside news sources that can help them fill the time. This system works much like the old school system of getting news updates via the News Wire.

One such service is called an audio news release (ANR) its a 60-second news story that includes a sound bite from you or your spokesperson that is approximately 20-seconds long. Radio Stations most often download audio from specialized radio content sites, which serve to feed them stories that may be of interest to the stations.

Benefits of an Audio News Release Service:

- Huge exposure to hundreds of stations.

- Morning Drive Time exposure - people listening on the way to work
- Huge Cost Savings - this is a FREE or Low cost opportunity
- Ability to localize a national story via localized sound bites.

Authors looking to take advantage of this service should look to work with a publicity company who understands how to use this very unique marketing method, and can help you create a plan that really works. Look in your area for publicity companies such as radio stations which may be willing to help for free or a low cost.

CHAPTER 9

TELEVISION MARKETING STRATEGIES

Many businesses find a well-crafted television advertisement gives them an effective way to appeal to their target market. However, the media can be expensive, since commercials need to run repeatedly to get the best results. Before you rush out to make your ad and book your spots, review the various marketing strategies available to help you produce the most effective, attention-grabbing ad possible.

Set Goals

The first strategy to implement in your television marketing plan is to identify the goals your want the commercials to achieve. For instance, your goal might include announcing a new product to your target market or increasing sales during a specific timeframe. Or you may want to use television commercials to build your brand so potential buyers get a good feeling about your business.

Go Local

If your market consists of people who live or work close to your business location, check with your local television station about running your ads during the two minutes of time per hour that most stations reserve for local advertisers. Start by identifying the programs that appeal to your target market and times at which these programs run. Then negotiate with the station to get the advertising slots you want that fit those programs and times. Offer to sign a long-term contract to get the best rates.

Encourage Action

After you spend fifteen to thirty seconds explaining the features and benefits of your product, make a strong call for action to encourage viewers to interact with your company. Provide your website address at the end of your ad to encourage viewers to get more information by visiting your website online. Provide a phone number so they can contact you via phone if necessary. Always provide at least three forms of contact. Usually these three forms of contact are: telephone, email and website domain. All three are important because each viewer may require a different approach. The purpose of your ad running is to give your company more exposure.

Direct Response

You may want more time to sell your products than the average commercial gives you. If so, consider direct response advertising strategies. The commercials include a strong call to action that focuses on asking viewer's to call an 800 number and place an order. The ads can run for up to thirty minutes. Direct response strategies are ideal for introducing new products so you can thoroughly explain the problem it solves as well as its features and benefits.

CHAPTER 10

RADIO MARKETING STRATEGIES

Advertising always entails some strategizing. Whether you are opting for a simple book marketing campaign or aiming for a more ambitious one, you need to have a strategy on hand to ensure the best results. Strategies are important because whenever one creates a goal, their strategy helps them to accomplish their goal. The same holds true when it comes to radio marketing advertising.

Author interviews are common among writers who wish to promote themselves to a massive audience. Unlike other types of advertising, which rely mostly on visuals to express their message, radio exclusively requires an audio presentation. They are usually easier to book and attend, and for such reason authors would not need to travel someplace else to conduct the interview. Instead, an author can opt to do a remote interview, interacting with thousands of listeners all from the privacy of their own homes.

Its relatively simple format does not mean however that you should be taking things easy when you do get invited on a radio show for your very first author interview. Any expert marketing consultant would advise you to do your homework first before taking advantage of advertising services. Similarly, you should first research about what it is you need to do before and during these kinds of events to ensure that you make a good impression on the listeners.

Take heed of the following hints:

You only have a short amount of time to express your message; in that period, you must be able to articulate whatever it is you want to say. Come up with a list of questions that your host or listener's may ask you and prepare your responses to them beforehand.

During call-in interviews, wherein people get to phone in and interact with you, remember to take down notes while your listeners are speaking. Write down their names and address them correctly when you respond to them. Be sure, though, to keep your answers short and sweet.

Provide your listeners with lots of information, but do not give them all the details. You do not want to leave them gasping for air from being overwhelmed with too much information. It is sufficient that you provide them with some good reasons why they should purchase your book.

How you project your voice is also essential during your interview. It is not enough to speak like how you usually do because your voice will not be able to carry over the airwaves and your message might get lost on your listeners. Speak in a slow and careful manner and be sure to add some inflection; at all costs, avoid being monotone.

Inform the host before the show if you have a personal website or blog through which your listener's can learn more about you. The host may choose to promote your site themselves during the segment, so you won't need to.

Conclude the interview by thanking the host and the producers for having you on their show. A handwritten thank-you note sent a day after the show is also a good idea; This helps to create a pleasant professional relationship with these people for networking purposes.

Radio is just one channel you can use in your aim to create some buzz about yourself and your work. There are many more marketing services out there which can work just as well for you.

CHAPTER 11

A STRATEGIC PR PLATFORM FOR SPONSORSHIPS, TV APPEARANCES AND OTHER EXPOSURE

Through book publishing, not only can anyone become an instant author, your book can be strategically leveraged to build toward more far-reaching marketing platforms than the internet. Craft your product as a multimedia communication tool for pitching your way to major offline opportunities, too. Then aim to get your book into the hands of decision-makers in high places and watch your business garden grow.

Imagine your own expansion possibilities, using this "Beyond-To" strategic exercise on how to get more from authoring ebooks: An Internet marketer goes BEYOND being a person few in his/her own city has heard of TO hosting a local radio show, thanks to the knowledge evidenced in a hot little PDF that tore across the Internet.

A small business owner or local artist goes BEYOND their traditional consumer confines TO writing a weekly newspaper column -- exponentially increasing their retail or art sales.

An aspiring motivational speaker goes BEYOND peddling a pricey audio CD series TO winning a small audience of executives at a major retail chain. The "bells and whistles" ebook leads to a sponsored tour of speaking engagements and leverages on going opportunities for you.

Whatever is your expertise -- be it gifts shop owner, avid traveler, motivational speaker, dating guru or super mom -- now is the time to give PDF "legs" to everything that you have learned. Optimize your effort by being strategic:

If you happen to be a blogger, you're ebook is probably already ninety percent written. Get an editor if you need to, to proofread and polish it.

If you are a business owner who's too busy to write, hire a ghost writer. But be sure to get one who will take the time to understand your story and insights and enhance your information through additional research.

Last but not least, if you are already marketing book, secure a public relations pro who's skilled at pitching corporate sponsorships, television segments, conference and convention planners, and more.

CHAPTER 12

BE PUBLISHED IN THE NEWSPAPER

Authors frequently turn to newspapers to market and advertise their offerings books because of the medium's ability to reach large numbers of people on a regular basis. But newspapers also have marketing needs to promote their brand, boost readership and take a competitive stance in the marketplace.

Newspaper Kiosks

Authors who are marketing their books can establish kiosks in well-traveled areas like shopping malls, post offices or train stations as a marketing strategy. Kiosks can sell current copies of the newspaper, but also provide customer services, such as subscription renewals, address changes and classified ad sales. Marketing tactic can include selling branded goods including canvas bags, hats or coffee cups with the newspaper logo.

Social Networking

Authors may use social networking to market the energy of the newsroom by creating accounts for individual reporters, photographers and editors to post story developments before the story; thus, allowing readers to post comments and questions for your newsroom employees to respond to, boosts interactivity and creates relationships between the public and your newspaper.

Contests and Freebies

Pairing contests with free copies of the newspaper is another useful marketing idea. Solicit current advertisers to sponsor contests for readers, providing recognition of their efforts in materials related to the contest, including contest guidelines printed in the newspaper and their logos featured on the contest webpage of your company site. Boost readership by soliciting essay submissions--for example, true courtship stories around Valentine's Day or scary story submissions near Halloween--and then publishing the stories on random days to encourage people to buy newspapers. Winner's can receive free subscriptions for a certain period of time.

Go Outside

Newspapers can market themselves by stepping outside the business world and extending a goodwill gesture to the community, with effects that resonate back to the office. For example, Kim Gordon, writing for Entrepreneur.com in an article entitled, "Fresh Ideas for Innovative Marketing," recommends purchasing the naming rights of a community hiking trail. Other ideas might include sponsoring a park bench, local beach break or scenic viewpoint. Periodically publish a newspaper story about your "adopted" location, such as its history or ecological challenges.

CHAPTER 13

SECRETS TO AFFILIATE MILLIONAIRES - 5 AFFILIATE MARKETING STRATEGIES FOR YOUR SUCCESS WITH LOW COST

Many studies show that there are a lot of free affiliate marketing strategies on the internet. However, the problem of most new affiliate marketing authors who have a limited budget is that they do not know exactly what strategies are workable and effective for their books. In this book, you will discover which affiliate marketing strategies are workable and proven that they are the most effective approaches. Also, you will learn how to start, build, run and grow your affiliate marketing business with those strategies as follows.

Free Affiliate Marketing Strategy 1: Place Online Classified Ads. Many experiences and research reveals that online classified ads are one of the most popular advertisements for buyers and sellers on the internet. If you have your own limited budget and would like to gear up the affiliate marketing books, placing online classified ads could be your choice. There are many well known online classified ads submission directories on the internet. The highest recommendation and the most popular site on the internet is the Craigslist directory. It is the global online classified ads submission directory; Craigslist directory is the most largest and popular site for placing an ads online now.

The secrets to affiliate millionaires for placing online classified ads to Craigslist are: (1) write your classified ads directly for your target audiences (2) include high performance keywords to maximize the benefits of searching (3) post your classified ads nearby the target (e.g. city, state and country) and (4) post often your ads on the Craigslist site.

Free Affiliate Marketing Strategy 2: Article Marketing

The article marketing has been proven that it is one of the best affiliate marketing strategies to drive high quality traffic and boost your affiliate commission. Actually, you will not pay any cents for this strategy if you learn and know the right way to approach this strategy properly. Many studies show that there are three categories you should consider for this strategy: (1) major and well-known article submission directory (2) minor article submission directory and (3) niche article submission websites. The highest recommendation for writing your articles and submitting your articles is to ensure that you submit all quality articles to those major and well-known submission sites. The characteristics of those major sties could be: (1) there is a lot of traffic and there are many proactive authors (2) there are many features supporting their authors and (3) there are a lot of potential partners.

The secrets to affiliate millionaires for writing articles are: (1) ensure that your articles are targeted to your audience with high quality and professional (2) include all high performance keywords to your articles and (3) write the most attractive article title.

Free Affiliate Marketing Strategy 3: Search Engine Optimization

Search engines play a major role for online business on the internet. There is no doubt that you should apply this strategy for running your affiliate marketing business. However, to apply this strategy, you have to build your own quality website. There are a lot of affordable and web hosting package out there to help you. Also, there are a lot of resources and guidelines for this strategy on the internet. In this section, you will discover and learn the highlight issues for maximizing the power of search engine optimization.

The secrets to affiliate millionaires for optimizing your website are: (1) insert all high performance keywords to your web page (e.g. META tag, title, header and body) (2) discover and generate niche keywords for your web page (3) write high relevancy and quality content to your high performance and niche keywords (4) ensure that you submit your website to well-known site and search engine submission directories and (5) exchange links among other websites.

Free Affiliate Marketing Strategy 4: Blogging Online Marketing.

Another affiliate marketing strategy you should consider for your success in the affiliate marketing business is to build up your own blog. Blog or web log is the most popular and fastest growing strategy for affiliate author's to grow their business. The greatest recommendations for blogging online are: (1) use your blog as a personal website to promote yourself and your business at the same time (2) use your blog as a review place for affiliate products and (3) contribute your works, news, information and servers in your blog as the community for your marketing strategies.

The secrets to affiliate millionaires for setting up your own blogs are: (1) post often the affiliate products review and buyer's guides (2) post often your personal messages to your customers or readers (3) advertise your blogs in multiple marketing channels (4) participant in the blog community and exchange comments among other blogs and (5) have a fun when you are using blogs to promote yourself and business.

Free Affiliate Marketing Strategy 5: Contextual Advertisement.

The contextual advertisement is another alternative affiliate marketing strategies to earn extra money for building, running and growing your affiliate marketing business. If you have truly limited budget and are looking for earning extra money to help your business, the contextual advertisement such as AdSense, Clicksor, and Auction Ads could be your choice.

The secrets to affiliate millionaires for earning extra money through those contextual advertisements are: (1) provide high quality and relevancy content (2) include high paying and performance keywords and (3) drive traffic to your content through multiple affiliate marketing strategies.

Final thoughts, you have learned how to start, build, run and grow your affiliate marketing business with low cost. With those above strategies, it will cost you only the web hosting package to get started. Also, you should run those strategies by steps: (1) place your online classified ads on Craigslist site (2) write and submit your articles to well-known article submission directory (3) optimize your web page (4) setup your own blog and promote yourself and (5) earn extra money through the contextual advertisements.

CHAPTER 14

TWENTY ECONOMICAL BOOK MARKETING TECHNIQUES

The succeeding book is about marketing self published books, profitable book marketing, book marketing strategies, and many other useful tips about online book marketing. Whether you are an upstart author or a self published author, an efficient book marketing plan need not be expensive if you just know your target market, find the most economical means to inform this market of your works, and establish a lasting, trustworthy relationship with your new-found markets.

Study carefully your expected demographic market's spending behavior and changing lifestyle habits, given these trying times, and then find effective ways and methods that they may be convinced and persuaded in buying your book. Also, compare the effectiveness of your book marketing plan with the competition of the same genre, and consider relevant marketing factors such as the pricing of the book, the common qualities of the bestselling authors, the present market demand for the genre, and the strengths and weaknesses of the competition. Try choosing or combining any of these effective book marketing techniques so that you will not only save on your book marketing investment but will become an efficient "author-preneur" as well:

1. Conduct book signing campaigns at local/statewide bookstores, book fairs, and literary conventions, which lets you market for free or for a very minimal registration fee.

2. Strategically schedule the announcement of your new book or continuing publicity with a relevant national news event or a trade fair.

3. Write articles on topics of current interest and correlate it with the beneficial features and advice found in your book, then submit at free PR websites.

4. Participate in various online authors' or genre-specific blog sites. This is one tried-and-tested avenue for the so-called "viral marketing" to flourish because in manifesting your thoughts and perspectives to thousands of online bloggers, you make them appreciate your knowledge and expertise on a particular subject matter of interest, which is related to the book you are writing. In this manner, you are actually and indirectly promoting your book with your interesting ideas shared online.

5. Publish actual portions or excerpts of your book together with a concise feature article that can be distributed in high visitor web portals and article data bases on the Internet.

6. Deal with a reliable print-on-demand publisher that offers complete and extensive distribution services.

7. Consider more promising, diversified literary text formatting options for your works like having a full text version of your book stored in pdf format, having an e-book version of your writing, and having downloadable versions of your book to Internet-capable handheld computer owners.

8. Participate often in writers' conventions, writing guild conferences and symposia and the like. You could gain crucial, practical inputs from seasoned authors who will give you effective marketing advice that may not be found elsewhere.

9. Have yourself available as a public forum/special events speaker in the field or area of your expertise. You may not actually sell books, but may issue author cards for the program participants who may be your future book buyers.

10. Consider listing your book on online classified ads websites.

11. Send e-mails to your friends and reader fans of scanned excerpts of your book with a matching explanatory note.

12. Place an ad in social networking sites that allow the marketing of your books/latest work for free or for a discounted fee.

13. Be a proactive author like giving complimentary copies of your book to celebrities and well-known resource persons, sending opinion articles for newspapers, and getting actively involved in community projects and charitable events.

14. Contact genre experts, independent book critics, and well known book review companies for favorable endorsement comments.

15. Send PR's to newspapers in your city or state for the purpose of being featured and getting book reviews.

16. Find local or state area radio stations and television stations that actually feature programs about writers, literature, or books then try to find out if you can send a PR of your book or better still, get a radio or television interview.

17. Make your own creative video presentation of your book and upload it to video-sharing websites.

18. Be your own book broadcaster. Make a podcast-able audio presentation of your book. This marketing option is ideal for author's of language and speech books, business and economics books, and even of the fiction genre.

19. Find author marketing websites that offer free ad listings of your book. This is the Internet version of the conventional bulletin board display.

20. Find book marketing services providers that offer bundled marketing programs at a discounted rate. Compare prices according to your book marketing needs, the kind of services that you prefer, the quality of the services offered, and the limits of your marketing budget.

CHAPTER 15

WHAT MAKES A GOOD BOOK MARKETER?

Whether you are a self published author or a book marketing services provider, it would be helpful to appreciate the importance of the following book marketing values and qualities in order for you to market more effectively:

Self-initiative. A good book marketer is proactive and does not fall into a false sense of complacency that the publishing industry will do all the marketing work for the book.

Being a good listener. A good book marketer welcomes ideas and suggestions from all sources, and is fair minded enough to find marketing wisdom from the pronouncements, including reader comments, genre experts' opinions, book critics' reviews, publishing industry executives' perspectives, and advice from book marketing services providers.

Being a good decision maker. A good book marketer knows how to determine which among the many book marketing options, both online and offline, will be effective in promoting his book. He knows how to find the right kind of balance from among the many marketing options presently available. He does not waste time on pursuing or insisting to market with futile and cumbersome practices that does not yield profitable sales income.

Being a practical business person. A good book marketer makes a sound marketing plan even while still in the process of writing the manuscript, and considers what could be effective marketing resources. The marketer also researches for effective, cost-efficient marketing options; studies the trends or in relation to reader preferences; and evaluates the success-failure ratio and effectiveness of the marketing options chosen. More specifically, the business-minded marketer also compares the book price, success factors of the genre competition: How did these authors market their book? Is the author concerned in a similar situation to also benefit from the success example, or are there factors that distinctly differentiate them thus calling for a totally different marketing plan?

Having versatile professional values. A good book marketer is multi-talented in every aspect and respect, endowed with certain worthy professional skills including the knowledge of an entrepreneur, the wisdom and sound advice of an expert, the inspiration of a motivational speaker, and the charm of an entertainer.

Resourcefulness and flexibility. A good book marketer accepts marketing failures in a constructive sense to find better and more effective means to promote the book.

Complete commitment. A good book marketer is committed to all aspects of the book marketing process, from start to finish, including the progress of the book promotion, and the evaluation of its effectiveness.

CHAPTER 16

FIVE SUCCESSFUL MARKETING STRATEGIES FOR FICTION AUTHOR'S

Through experience, I've found that marketing fiction is a different beast to marketing non-fiction. The "platform" is still important, but in a different way and other things make more of a difference to direct sales.

Get A Professional Book Cover Design

Cover design might sound like a publishing exercise, but your book cover is also critical for marketing. If you manage to get millions of eyeballs onto your book sales page and your cover is terrible, nobody will sample, let alone buy. If you pitch a book blogger, a journalist or a physical bookstore owner, one glance at the book cover will determine their interest. So this is a non-negotiable upfront task, along with professional editing to ensure you have a quality product.

Non-fiction book covers have a trend for large words, focusing on the obvious benefit for the customer. But fiction book covers need to resonate with your target market, echoing the genre of the book and giving a taste for the story. You can also help the design process. Go into the Amazon store and look at the Top 100 books for the genre you are writing in. Notice what is similar about the bestselling books and take screen-prints to share with your designer. If you are unsure about your genre, pick 3-5 books or authors that your book is like and see where they are categorized. This one tip will also carry into much of your other marketing, so it is critical to the process. Your book is never totally unique, nor do you want it to be, because you want to find an existing readership and tap into that.

As well as the book cover design, you need a compelling sales description, targeted categories, well-researched keywords, good reviews and appropriate pricing. Basically, the book sales sites will always be able to sell more books than you can so you want to make sure you optimize your book page.

Build your own email list of fans and use paid promotion for sales spikes book marketing; The best way to send your book to the top of the sales charts is to email your own list of fans. You can grow this specific list for your fiction by including a link at the end of your books.

For non-fiction authors and online businesses, you can grow your list on your own website by offering something for free and attracting attention and traffic with content marketing.

Fiction readers mainly find books on the actual book sales sites, like Amazon, Kobo, iBookstore, etc., so your main method of capture is at the end of your book. Discovering this changed my own mindset.

Of course, it takes a while to grow your own email list and one of the best tactics for short-term sales spikes right now is to pay for a promotional service which already has a huge list of readers ready to buy. These sites and services will change over time, so always assess the evidence for anything you decide to participate in. But if you have good reviews and a great cover, plus you can drop your price for a sale, this type of promotion can work well for a short-term sales spike.

Solicit reviews from customers and book bloggers. There are two types of reviews, both of which can be effective for fiction book marketing.

Customer reviews on Amazon, Goodreads and the other booksites. These feed into the algorithms that determine how your book fares on the various lists and also have an impact on visibility. They provide social proof on the book sales page so more customers will buy. One way to get reviews is to build an email list (as above) and give them books for free. But you should also be including a notice at the back of your book, thanking people for reading and asking nicely for a review. Linking to the sales page is a good way to redirect them back to it.

Reviews by book bloggers and other media. These can help generate word of mouth sales by bringing your book to the notice of avid readers in a genre. Because many of the bloggers read each other's sites, you can also end up featuring on a number of blogs. Pitching book bloggers takes time because you have to focus on researching the ones that will like your kind of book.

Collaboration and co-opetition book marketing; There are people who say social media and 'platform' are a waste of time when it comes to selling fiction. I agree that it is less effective for direct sales than for non-fiction; however, I still think it is essential for longer term marketing.

Co-opetition means co-operating with your 'competition' for mutual benefit. Fiction readers are often voracious, finishing a favorite author's latest book in just a few hours. We can never satisfy a reader's appetite for books alone, so it's a great idea to work with other authors in the same genre to promote books that those readers will like. There has been a rise in multi-author blogs for fiction, multi-book box-sets of ebooks in the Kindle store and promotion of each other on social media.

So all the platform tactics are useful, but the focus should be more on longer term branding, connections and ways to reach readers in a genre by working with other similar authors, rather than immediate, direct sales.

Write More Fiction, Of Varying Lengths.

Probably the best way to sell more fiction is to write more fiction! More digital shelf space means more visibility, and often the best way to sell more books is to launch a new one that can bring more readers to your backlist. Of course, this takes time, so many authors are also playing with novellas and short story collections to entice readers with great content that does not take so long to write and produce. If you have work of different lengths, you can also play with pricing models and promotional sales, which is difficult to do with one book.

CHAPTER 17

COMMON MISTAKES AUTHORS MAKE ON INSTAGRAM

Key to any great social media strategy is understanding the core values and tools available on each individual social platform. Different platforms have different pros and cons, uses, and effects on your book promotion. It's important that you take the time to learn which strategies and content perform best on the platforms that you choose to use. Content created without strategy or purpose is not worthy of being posted on your author platform channels. There are some authors on Instagram posting content that belongs on a different platform. Instagram may be owned by Facebook, but as platforms they are extremely different. Ask Yourself: Do I know the ins and outs of Instagram strategy? Do I feel confident about how best to use this app for book marketing?

2 – NOT UNDERSTANDING WHAT TO POST AND WHY

Instagram is a platform designed for visual storytelling. You may know to how craft a story on paper, but in order to best promote that physical work you need to understand how to craft a story on social media. Social media platforms like Instagram are incredible tools you can use to connect with and convert potential readers, tools that are under utilized when an author does not understand the shift to digital content creation.

3 – USING HASHTAGS INCORRECTLY

Do you often feel confused about how hashtags work and which ones to use? If you are using hashtags that are irrelevant to your subject, without checking their activity, or creating hashtags of your own invention, then you are doing something wrong. Instead, you need to use hashtags that are relevant, timely, and searchable. Hashtags are used to create categories on the platform and increase the likelihood of your posts being seen and therefore engaged with. Take a look at the last set of hashtags you used on your Instagram posts. Are they serving your content well? If not, reconsider your hashtag choices.

4 – LACK OF AUDIENCE TARGETING & COMMUNITY BUILDING

Instagram is a platform used by millions of individuals with thousands of different interests and desires which create dedicated communities, like readers and book bloggers. The question becomes, how do you reach the community that will serve your book marketing best? How do your reach your target audience on Instagram?

If your content on Instagram isn't attracting the right users with the right interests then all of your social media efforts are wasted. You need to create content with a strategy in mind, content that is relevant to your target audience, their interests and desires. Ask yourself: "Who is my target audience?" You may also ask yourself: "Am I creating content that interests and attracts them?"

5 – FAILED COMMUNITY BUILDING

One of the biggest benefits of Instagram is the incredible potential for community building. You can use social media as part of your author platform to build a dedicated following that is not only interested in you and your work, but excited to be a part of it. Too many authors misuse or misunderstand community building techniques and strategies, failing to create a community that will support the sale of their books time and time again.

Consider this: would you rather have 1,000 followers who never engage on your posts and never show any interest in what you do? OR would you rather have 1,000 followers who are excited to see what you are working on next, who cannot wait to buy your next book and share it with their friends? The answer is clear. If you have followers, but not a community, then something is wrong with your author social media strategy. You have work and implement different strategies; Your followers should be your community.

CHAPTER 18

WHAT'S NEXT?

It's like the new "fill-in-the-blank" marketing term that makes you sound all smartish. Yes! Content Marketing is all of that and more. But, mostly it's about strategy. You will find a lot of definitions of content marketing and pretty much all of them will center around the idea of creating quality content with the purpose of persuading a defined audience to buy from you - without being annoying and salesy.

Yes, you need good content, but there is something that most personality entrepreneurs (i.e. speakers, authors, coaches.etc) like you are not told. Newsflash! Most of the content marketing advice, articles and tips are not for you...

Okay then who is it for?

It is easy to Google content marketing and find all kinds of eyeopening articles that show you how to grow your business with content. But, it is also easy for busy entrepreneurs like you to get overwhelmed and confused by information you do not have the time, or resources to put into motion.

Breaking The Curse Of The Busy Solo-Preneur

Content Savvy & Successful Tip! Do not invest in copy-writing courses and templates if you know you hate to write. It is just a waste of precious time and money. I see this a lot. You become desperate, because your business is stalled due to lack of communication. You need to blog more and communicate with your list more.

You hate writing, but you know you need content. So, you purchase a bunch of PLR and copy-writing products that aim to help make writing easy and fast. The problem is you still hate or lack the time to write, so that stuff you bought is just collecting dust on your hard drive.

As a result, many of us spend most of our time building million dollar hard-drives versus million dollar businesses. It is really not your fault. You're just doing what you gotta do to move your business forward. The key to breaking this curse and bad investments is to always keep a high level view of your business. Don't get lost in the details that matter, but you may not good at. This will help you to stay focused and keep you from burning out in areas you're passionate in, because you have over indulged in other stuff. Trying to become an expert copywriter or marketing strategist when your gift is in teaching people public speaking, will undoubtedly have you feeling like you don't know what business in anymore.

What You Need to Know About Content + Marketing to Make Your Marketing Easier and More Effective...

Many entrepreneurs get caught up in trying to write killer headlines and cookie-cutter templates. But, in the hands of the busy entrepreneur it's just a recipe for overwhelm & mediocre pie. Do not be afraid to ask for help; to delegate the services which you need.

If you are anything like me, you have read this book and still asked yourself: "Um, ok. What's next?"

UM OKAY, SO WHAT'S NEXT?

Next, you should use all the information provided in the book. Make sure you have your social media pages created, and that you are posting weekly at the minimum.

Next, go to your local library. Donate a book. You can have your book available in any library free of cost; all you must do is donate a book. Why not make a visit to your local library? Ask about booking a room, normally this fee is low cost for patrons. You may use the room for various purposes such as a reading day, or a book signing. Make sure you book the date and create invites for the occasion.

Are you still wondering: what's next? Determine your audience. Next, Google, call, and email schools, church facilities, universities, colleges after selecting which may be of a good resourse. Make resourceful decision-making people aware of your book and leverage yourself as a speaker. If you use Google, you can pull up any student services department for a college or university. Use this information, send an email which include an excpert of your book, your biography and website link. Guess what? All this information can be submitted electronically online, so you just saved yourself thousands of dollars in printing while still achieving marketing goals. Select schools, church facilities, universities, colleges based on which audience your book appeals to the most.

A great way to do this on the collegiate level is to visit this website: www.naca.org The National Association for Campus Activities (NACA) is a recognized source because NACA provides knowledge, ideas and resources for campus life. If you are an author, musician or entertainer of some sort, you may register for a fee on this website. NACA offers opportunities for growth through social events and your information will be showcased to colleges, and universities which may be seeking to bring in published authors in as speakers. Each college or university has a student services department; student services select different forms of educational entertainment for students. Why not you? So, go for it. Register your information, pay the fee which is reasonable and market yourself as a speaker. Before doing this, you should have followed previous steps of having a website, business cards, etc.

What's next? Contact your local news or radio station via phone, or email; this information will be available on the company's website. Rather you email, call or both, make them aware of your new publication and that you would love to come on to be interviewed. As mentioned earlier, have your questions (PR Packet) prior to gaining interview.

Don't stop at your local news stations because you do not want to limit yourself to just one area. Look in nearby towns and cities. Submit your book and information ongoing. Be creative and share your information. While a lot of new channels will promote by conducting an interview, they may not pay. That's okay because you are still getting publicity which will enhance your career overall, so go for it.

What's next? The sky has no limit. One of my most liked quotes is one by Madam C.J. Walker: "Don't sit and wait for opportunities to come. You have to get up and make them!" All that we have discussed is centered of the fact that if you are not only going to be a published author but be a successful author you must become ambitioned enough to put your product out there. We have offered many strategies to help you along the way.

www.ingramcontent.com/pod-product-compliance
Lightning Source LLC
LaVergne TN
LVHW051210080426
835512LV00019B/3184